WITHDRAWN

GREEN SONG AND OTHER POEMS

Books by Edith Sitwell

STREET SONGS
A POET'S NOTEBOOK
PLANET AND GLOW-WORM

GREEN SONG

&

OTHER POEMS

BY

EDITH SITWELL

LONDON
MACMILLAN & CO. LTD
1944

PRINTED IN GREAT BRITAIN
BY R. & R. CLARK, LIMITED, EDINBURGH

TO BRYHER

ACKNOWLEDGMENTS

MY thanks are due to the Editors of *The Times Literary Supplement*, *Life and Letters To-Day*, *New Writing and Daylight*, the 'Penguin' *New Writing*, and the *Atlantic Monthly* for permission to reprint poems first published by them.

My thanks are also due to Messrs. Gerald Duckworth for permission to reprint certain lines which first appeared in my *Selected Poems*, published by them, and which I have now used in 'One Day in Spring', and 'Lo, this is she that was the World's Desire'.

E. S.

CONTENTS

CONTENTS

Heart and Mind

SAID the Lion to the Lioness — ' When you are amber
    dust, —
No more a raging fire like the heat of the Sun
(No liking but all lust) —
Remember still the flowering of the amber blood and
    bone
The rippling of bright muscles like a sea,
Remember the rose-prickles of bright paws
Though we shall mate no more
Till the fire of that sun the heart and the moon-cold bone
    are one.'

Said the Skeleton lying upon the sands of Time —
' The great gold planet that is the mourning heat of the
    Sun
Is greater than all gold, more powerful
Than the tawny body of a Lion that fire consumes
Like all that grows or leaps . . . so is the heart
More powerful than all dust.   Once I was Hercules
Or Samson, strong as the pillars of the seas :
But the flames of the heart consumed me, and the mind
Is but a foolish wind.'

Said the Sun to the Moon — ' When you are but a lonely
    white crone,
And I, a dead King in my golden armour somewhere in a
    dark wood,
Remember only this of our hopeless love
That never till Time is done
Will the fire of the heart and the fire of the mind be one.'

Green Song

TO DAVID HORNER

AFTER the long and portentous eclipse of the patient sun
The sudden spring began
With the bird-sounds of Doom in the egg, and Fate in
    the bud that is flushed with the world's fever —
But those bird-songs have trivial voices and sound not
    like thunder,
And the sound when the bud bursts is no more the sound
    of the worlds that are breaking.—
But the youth of the world, the lovers, said, ' It is Spring !
And we who were black with the winter's shade, and old,
See the emeralds are awake upon the branches
And grasses, bird-blood leaps within our veins
And is changed to emeralds like the sap in the grasses.
The beast-philosopher hiding in the orchards,
Who had grown silent from the world's long cold
Will tell us the secret of how Spring began
In the young world before the Fall of Man.
For you are the young spring earth
And I, O Love, your dark and lowering heaven.'

But an envious ghost in the spring world
Sang to them a shrunken song
Of the world's right and wrong —
Whispered to them through the leaves, ' I wear
The world's cold for a coat of mail
Over my body bare —
I have no heart to shield my bone
But with the world's cold am alone —
And soon your heart, too, will be gone —
My day's darling.'

The naked Knight in the coat of mail
Shrieked like a bird that flies through the leaves —
The dark bird proud as the Prince of the Air,
' I am the world's last love. . . . Beware —

Young girl, you press your lips to lips
That are already cold —
For even the bright earthly dress
Shall prove, at last, unfaithfulness.

His country's love will steal his heart —
To you it will turn cold
When foreign earth lies on the breast
Where your young heart was wont to rest
Like leaves upon young leaves, when warm was the green
    spray,
And warm was the heart of youth, my day's darling.

And if that ghost return to you —
(The dead disguised as a living man)
Then I will come like Poverty
And wear your face, and give your kiss,
And shrink the world, and that sun the heart
Down to a penny's span :

For there is a sound you heard in youth,
A flower whose light is lost —
There is a faith and a delight —
They lie at last beneath my frost
When I am come like Time that all men, faiths, loves,
    suns defeat,
My frost despoils the day's young darling.

For the young heart like the spring wind grows cold
And the dust, the shining racer, is overtaking
The laughing young people who are running like fillies
The golden ladies and the ragpickers
And the foolish companions of spring, the wild wood
    lilies.'

But the youth of the world said, ' Give me your golden
    hand
That is but earth, yet it holds the lands of heaven

And you are the sound of the growth of spring in the
     heart's deep core,
The hawthorn-blossoming boughs of the stars and the
     young orchards' emerald lore.'

And hearing that, the poor ghost fled like the winter
     rain —
Sank into greenish dust like the fallen moon
Or the sweet green dust of the lime-flowers that will be
     blossoming soon —
And spring grew warm again —

No more the accusing light, revealing the rankness of
     Nature,
All motives and desires and lack of desire
In the human heart, but loving all life, it comes to bless
Immortal things in their poor earthly dress —
The blind of life beneath the frost of their great winter
And those for whom the winter breaks in flower
And summer grows from a long-shadowed kiss.
And Love is the vernal equinox in the veins
When the sun crosses the marrow and pith of the heart
Among the veridian smells, the green rejoicing.
All names, sounds, faiths, delights, and duties lost
Return to the hearts of men, those households of high
     heaven.
And voices speak in the woods as from a nest
Of leaves — they sing of rest,
And love, and toil, the rhythms of their lives,
Singing how winter's dark was overcome,
And making plans for tomorrow as though yesterday
Had never been, nor the lonely ghost's old sorrow,
And Time seemed but the beat of heart to heart,
And Death the pain of earth turning to spring again
When lovers meet after the winter rain.
And when we are gone, they will see in the great
     mornings
Born of our lives, some memory of us, the golden stalk

Of the young long-petalled flower of the sun in the pale
    air
Among the dew. . . . Are we not all of the same substance,
Men, planets and earth, born from the heart of darkness,
Returning to darkness, the consoling mother,
For the short winter sleep — O my calyx of the flower of
    the world, you the spirit
Moving upon the waters, the light on the breast of the
    dove.

Anne Boleyn's Song

'AFTER the terrible rain, the Annunciation' —
The bird-blood in the veins that has changed to emeralds
Answered the bird-call. . . .
In the neoteric Spring the winter coldness
Will be forgotten
As I forget the coldness of my last lover,

The great grey King
Who lies upon my breast
And rules the bird-blood in my veins that shrieked with
    laughter
— A sound like fear —
When my step light and high
Spurned my sun down from the sky
In my heedless headless dance —
O many a year ago, my dear,
My living lass !

In the nights of Spring, the bird, the Angel of the
    Annunciation
Broods over his heaven of wings and of green wild-fire
That each in its own world, each in its egg
Like Fate is lying.

He sang to my blood, as Henry, my first King,
My terrible sun
Came like the Ethos of Spring, the first green streak,
And to me cried,
'Your veins are the branches where the first blossom
    begins
After the winter rains —
Your eyes are black and deep
As the prenatal sleep
And your arms and your breasts are my Rivers of Life
While a new world grows in your side.'

Men said I was the primal Fall,
That I gave him the world of spring and of youth like an
    apple
And the orchards' emerald lore —
And sin lay at the core.

But Henry thought me winter-cold
When to keep his love I turned from him as the world
Turns from the sun . . . and then the world grew old —

But I who grew in the heart as the bird-song
Grows in the heart of Spring . . . I, terrible Angel
Of the emeralds in the blood of man and tree,
How could I know how cold the nights of Spring would
    be

When my grey glittering King —
Old amorous Death grew acclimatised to my coldness :
His age sleeps on my breast,
My veins, like branches where the first peach-blossom
Trembles, bring the Spring's warmth to his greyness.

A Young Girl

Is it the light of the snow that soon will be overcoming
The spring of the world ?   Ah no, the light is the white-
  ness of all the wings of the angels
As pure as the lily born with the white sun.
And I would that each hair on my head was an angel,
  O my red Adam,
And my neck could stretch to you like a sunbeam or the
  young shoot of a lily
In the first spring of the world, till you, my grandeur of
  clay,
My Adam, red loam of the orchard, forgetting
The thunders of wrongs and of rights and of ruins
Would find the green shadow of spring beneath the hairs
  of my head, those bright angels,
And my face, the white sun that is born of the stalk of a
  lily
Come back from the underworld, bringing light to the
  lonely :
Till the people in islands of loneliness cry to the other
  islands
Forgetting the wars of men and of angels, the new Fall of
  Man.

Harvest

TO STEPHEN SPENDER

I, AN old woman whose heart is like the Sun
That has seen too much, looked on too many sorrows,
Yet is not weary of shining, fulfilment and harvest
Heard the priests that howled for rain and the universal
    darkness,
Saw the golden princes sacrificed to the Rain-god,
The cloud that came, and was small as the hand of Man.
And now in the time of the swallow, the bright one, the
    chatterer,
The young women wait like the mother of corn for the
    lost one —
Their golden eyelids are darkened like the great rain-clouds.
But in bud and branch the nature of Fate begins
— And Love with the Lion's claws and the Lion's hunger
Hides in the brakes in the nihilistic Spring.—
Old men feel their scolding heart
Reproach the veins that for fire have only anger.
And Christ has forgiven all men — the thunder-browed
    Caesar
That stone-veined Tantalus howling with thirst in the plain
Where for innocent water flows only the blood of the slain,
Falling for ever from veins that held in their noonday
The foolish companion of summer, the weeping rose.
We asked for a sign that we have not been forsaken —
And for answer the Abraham-bearded Sun, the father of
    all things
Is shouting of ripeness over our harvest for ever.
And with the sound of growth, lion-strong, and the
    laughing Sun
Whose great flames stretch like branches in the heat
Across the firmament, we almost see
The great gold planets spangling the wide air
And earth —
        O sons of men, the firmament's belovèd,
The Golden Ones of heaven have us in care —

9   G.S.—B

With planetary wisdom, changeless laws,
Ripening our lives and ruling hearts and rhythms,
Immortal hungers in the veins and heart
Born from the primal Cause
That keeps the hearts and blood of men and beasts ever
    in motion,
The amber blood of the smooth-weeping tree
Rising toward the life-giving heat of the Sun. . . .
For is not the blood, — the divine, the animal heat
That is not fire, — derived from the solar ray ?
And does not the Beast surpass all elements
In power, through the heat and wisdom of the blood
Creating other Beasts — the Lion a Lion, the Bull a Bull
The Bear a Bear — some like great stars in the rough
And uncreated dark — or unshaped universes
With manes of fire and a raging sun for heart.
Gestation, generation and duration —
The cycles of all lives upon the earth —
Plants, beasts and men, must follow those of heaven :
The rhythms of our lives
Are those of the ripening, dying of the seasons,
Our sowing and reaping in the holy fields,
Our love and giving birth — then growing old
And sinking into sleep in the maternal
Earth, mother of corn, the wrinkled darkness.
So we, ruled by those laws, see their fulfilment.
And I who stood in the grave-clothes of my flesh
Unutterably spotted with the world's woes
Cry, ' I am Fire.   See, I am the bright gold
That shines like a flaming fire in the night — the gold-
    trained planet,
The laughing heat of the Sun that was born from dark-
    ness —
Returning to darkness — I am fecundity, harvest.'
For on each country road
Grown from the needs of men as boughs from trees,
The reapers walk like the harvesters of heaven —
Jupiter and his great train, and the corn-goddess,

And Saturn marching in the Dorian mode.
We heard in the dawn the first ripe-bearded fire
Of wheat (so flames that are men's spirits break from
    their thick earth).
Then came the Pentecostal Rushing of Flames, God in
    the wind that comes to the wheat,
Returned from the Dead for the guilty hands of Caesar
Like the rose at morning shouting of red joys
And redder sorrows fallen from young veins and heart-
    springs,
Come back for the wrong and the right, the wise and the
    foolish
Who like the rose care not for our philosophies
Of life and death, knowing the earth's forgiveness
And the great dews that come to the sick rose :
For those who build great mornings for the world
From Edens of lost light seen in each other's eyes,
Yet soon must wear no more the light of the Sun,
But say farewell among the morning sorrows.
The universal language of the Bread —
(O Thou who are not broken, nor divided —
Thou who art eaten, but like the Burning Bush
Art not consumed — Thou Bread of Men and Angels —
The Seraphim rank on rank of the ripe wheat —
Gold-bearded thunders and hierarchies of heaven
Roar from the earth : ' Our Christ is arisen, He comes to
    give a sign from the Dead.'

Song

' O DIONYSUS of the tree — you of the beard, you of the
  ripeness
Among the branches of my arms and hair
As the boughs of the vine hold the plane-tree —
You came like the wind in the branches.'

' And to the earth of my heart, O golden woman
You are the corn-goddess.'

' O wind, come again to my branches.'

' O darkness of earth — O ripeness.'

One Day in Spring

GONE is the winter's cold
In the wild wood and the heart —
And warm are the young leaves and the budding spray.
' O heart, O eyes, O lips that will grow not old,
The waters love the moon, the sun the day,
As I love you, my day's darling ! '

Said the youth of the world.   But a living dead man walked
In the spring fire and talked
As if one heard him,—though in all the spring
No heart was listening.
(' O heed him not, my dew with golden feet
Flying from me, my dew that is born of the spring heat.')

' On that last day she said, " I shall be cold
To the world's end, without your kiss . . . but when
    Death is so old
He no more feels the pain
Of jealous love, I shall be yours again.

On that great holiday
There'll be no work, no fear for tomorrow's bread
Nor will the nations rage —
And only Death will feel the sorrow of old age."

Then, Sun of my life, she went to warm the Dead,
And I must now go sunless in their stead.

I felt not the cold wind blow,—
Nor the change of the sun :
For earth and sea
And my heart were one :
There nothing grew ; they nothing knew
Except the world was done !

They clothed a dead man in my dress
Who rose in the morning sorrow —

And all day walked the earth, waving at Nothingness
Now high, now low —
Changing with every wind like a scarecrow.

Sometimes my voice would sound from those dead lips :
For I who had seen
Each stain of age, fatigue, upon her cheek —
Dimming her beauty — I who had feared to see
That eternal truth the Bone
Laid bare by Death — cried now " Come home ! — what-
    ever stain
Death laid upon you, in whatever guise,
You are now, I should know your heart ! Come home,
    out of the rain,

The cold ! How shall I bear my heart without its beat,
— My clay without its soul ? . . . I am alone —
More cold than you are in your grave's long night,
That has my heart for covering, warmth and light."

The cathedrals and their creeds were built above
Her heart. And all the Babels of the world,
Their bells and madness tolled — " Dead " — over her
    love . . .
But the earth and all the roots of trees in the winter earth
Yet could not hold her down —
The tides of seas and seasons could not drown

Her heart. . . . So after twelve months in her grave
She came to me and gave
Her kiss . . . humbly and pleadingly she crept beside
My bed and looked at me with those hollow eyes
That seemed as if they had wept
For the stains Death left upon her beauty, fearing I might
Love her no more — so she came home from her endless
    night

— And the lips of my dead love were warm to me.
But the lips, the heart, should be dust-dun, death-cold
From that long night . . . and so I feared to hold
That heart that came warm from the grave . . . afraid
Of that eternity of love I laid
Death's earth upon her heart; for this
Dead man in my dress dared not kiss
Her who laid by Death's cold lest I
Should feel it when she came to lie
Upon my heart . . . my dead love gave
Lips warm with love though from her grave :
And I gave Death her love — the only light
And fire she had to warm her eternal night.'

So he went by.   The snowflake's star can see
Its ephemeral cold in the eternity

Of the rock-crystal's six rays . . . so light grief and
     waterfalls
See that eternal grief that melts not though the last spring
     calls

The heart. . . . But where the wild birds sing
We walked together
And pitied the poor Dead for whom the Spring
Is cold . . . for all the strange green fire
In eyes, on hair, — the world, the veins, changed into
     emeralds.

O Dead, your heart is gone ! you cannot weep ;
And like the unborn child's should be your sleep.

But on your lips, long worn away, a youthful smile
Remains, a thing of sorrow —

And wasted so thin by hopeless love you seem a shade —
An echo only —

You wait for one who comes not, for the hour
When your lips spoke, and winter broke in flower,

The Parthenon was built by your dead kiss . . .
But what should love seek now you are changed to this

Thin piteous wreck ! — yet strong as the Prophet's rock
No grief tears waters from that stone to mock

Death's immobility — and changed to stone
Those eyelids see one sight, and one alone.

What do they see ?   Some lost and childish kiss
In summer, in the dews of a dead morning —
The meeting, and clasp of hands, the last farewell
Among the morning sorrows ?   Now in spring

Beneath the young green-blooming strawberry
In the deep groves they sigh for the forgotten bliss
Grown dead and rotten, of their lover's kiss,
Forgetting the young heart grows old
And in the spring night they must sleep alone.

But in the spring warmth, creatures, faiths and men
Awaken in the sun —
The coldness of the heart
Is with the winter done —

And the waters love the moon, the sun the day —
As I love my day's darling.

Though all the lovers of the world
Grow old, and fade, and die —
Yet how should you and I ?
For the world was only made that we should love —
O hair, O eyes, O lips that will never grow old !

Invocation

FOR ALEC AND MERULA GUINNESS

I who was once a golden woman like those who walk
In the dark heavens — but am now grown old
And sit by the fire, and see the fire grow cold,
Watch the dark fields for a rebirth of faith and of wonder.

The turning of Ixion's wheel the day
Ceased not, yet sounds no more the beat of the heart
But only the sound of ultimate Darkness falling
And of the Blind Samson at the Fair, shaking the pillars
    of the world and emptily calling.

For the gardeners cried for rain, but the high priests
    howled
For a darker rain to cool the delirium of gold
And wash the sore of the world, the heart of Dives,
Raise wheat for the hunger that lies in the soul of the
    poor —
Then came the thunderous darkness

And the fly-like whispering of small hopes, small fears,
The gossips of mean Death — gadflies and gnats, the
    summer world :
The small and gilded scholars of the Fly
That feed upon the crowds and their dead breath
And buzz and stink where the bright heroes die
Of the dust's rumours and the old world's fevers.
Then fell the world in winter.

But I, a golden woman like the corn goddess
Watch the dark fields, and know when spring begins
To the sound of the heart and the planetary rhythm,
Fires in the heavens and in the hearts of men,
Young people and young flowers come out in the
    darkness.

And where are they going ?   How should I know ?   I
    see only
The hierarchies love the young people — the Swan has
    given his snows
And Berenice her wild mane to make their fair hair,
And speaking of love are the voices that come from the
    darkness :

Of the nobler love of Man for his brother Man,
And of how the creeds of the world shall no more divide
    them
But every life be that of a country Fate
Whose wheel had a golden woof and warp, the Day —
Woven of threads of the common task ; and light
Tells to that little child the humble dust
Tales of the old world's holiness, finds veins of ore
In the unripe wheat-ear ; and the common fire
That drops with seed like the Sun's, is fallen from the
    long-leaved planets.

So when the winter of the world and Man's fresh Fall
When democratic Death feared no more the heart's
    coldness
Shall be forgotten,
O Love, return to the dying world, as the light
Of morning, shining in all regions, latitudes
And households of high heaven within the heart.

Be then our visible world, our world invisible !
Throughout our day like the laughing flames of the Sun
Lie on our leaves of life, your heat infusing
Deep in the amber blood of the smooth tree.
The panic splendour of the animal
Is yours — O primal Law
That rules the blood (the solar ray in the veins) —
The fire of the hearth, the household Deity
That shines not, nor does it burn, destroy like fire,
But nourishes with its endless wandering
Like that of the Golden Ones in the high heavens.

Rule then the spirit working in dark earth
As the Sun and Planets rule the husbandman —
O pride that in each semitone
Of amber blood and bone
Proclaims the splendour that arose from the first Dark !

Be too the ear of wheat to the Lost Men
Who ask the city stones if they are bread
And the stones of the city weep. . . .
                                        You, the lost days
When all might still be hoped for, and the light
Laid gold in the unhopeful path of the poor —
The shrunken darkness in the miser's heart.

Now falls the night of the world : — O Spirit moving upon
        the waters
Your peace instil
In the animal heat and splendour of the blood —
The hot gold of the sun that flames in the night
And knows not down-going
But moves with the revolutions in the heavens.

The thunders and the fires and acclamations
Of the leaves of spring are stilled, but in the night
The Holy Ghost speaks in the whispering leaves.
O wheat-ear shining like a fire and the bright gold,
O water brought from far to the dying gardens !

Bring peace to the famine of the heart and lips,
And to the Last Man's loneliness
Of those who dream they can bring back sight to the blind !
You are the Night
When the long hunt for Nothing is at rest
In the Blind Man's Street, and in the human breast
The hammer of Chaos is stilled.
                                        Be then the sleep
When Judas gives again the childish kiss
That once his mother knew — and wash the stain
From the darkened hands of the universal Cain.

'O bitter love, O Death . . .'

I DREW a stalk of dry grass through my lips
And heard it sigh
'Once I was golden Helen . . . but am now a thin
Dry stalk of quaking grass. . . . What wind, what Paris
    now would win
My love ? — for I am drier than a crone.'

But the sap in those dry veins sang like a bird :
' I was the sea that knew the siren song
And my veins heard
A planet singing in the Dorian mode ! '

An old man weary with rolling wisdom like a stone
Up endless hills to lay on the innocent eyes
Said, ' Once I was Plato, wise
In the ripe and unripe weathers of the mind,
And I could draw

The maps of worlds beyond the countries of the blind
Sense ; I found the law
Uniting atoms of our Chaos like the love
Of boy and girl.'

               Another old man said
' I was a great gold-sinewed King, I had a lion's mane
Like the raging Sun . . . but now I am alone —
And my love, that white lady, is but a thin white bone.

I live in my perpendicular grey house
Then in my horizontal house — a foolish bed
For one whose blood like Alexander roamed
Conquering the countries of the heart.
                    All is the same :
The heroes marched like waves upon the shore :

Their great horizons, and the kiss
Of lovers, and of atoms, end in this.'

O bitter love, O Death that came
To steal all that I own.

' Lo, this is she that was the world's desire '

In the green winter night
That is dark as the cypress bough, the pine,
The fig-tree and the vine
When our long sun into the dark had set
And made but winter branches of his rays
The heart, a ghost,
Said to our life farewell — the shadow leaves
The body when our long dark sun has gone. . . .

And this is the winter's Aethiopian clime,
Darkening all beauty. . . .
                              Now in the winter night
The seed of the fire
Fallen from the long-leaved planets is of gold.
But she is old
And no more loved by the stars. . . . O now no more
The gold kiss of Orion burns her cheek.

Grey dust bent over the fire in the winter night,
Was this the crone that once Adonis loved,

Were those the veins that heard the sirens' song ?
Age shrinks her heart to dust, black as the Ape's
And shrunk and cold
Is Venus now, grown blackened, noseless, old !

So changed is she by Time's appalling night
That even her bone can no more stand upright

But leans as if it thirsted — for what spring ?
The Ape's bent skeleton foreshadowing

With head bent from the light, its only kiss.
Now she, too, knows the metamorphosis

When the appalling lion-claws of age
With talons tear the cheek and heart, yet rage

For life devours the bone, a tigerish fire :
The craters in the heart weep to that mire
The flesh . . . but the long wounds torn by Time in the
    golden cheek
Seem the horizons of the endless cold.
Lo, this is she that was the world's desire.

Crouched by the fire, blind from her earth's thick hood
Of dust, she, Atridae-like, devours her blood

With hopeless love, and knows the anguish of the bone
Deserted by all love, with Death alone.

And now the small immortal serpent cries,
' To my embrace the foolish and the wise

Will come,' and the first soundless wrinkles fall like snow
On many a golden cheek, and none may know

Seeing the ancient wrinkled shadow-shape
If this be long-dead Venus, or the Ape

Our great precursor. . . .
                          I felt pity for the dust,
And Time, the earth from which our beauty grows,
The old unchanging memory of the bone —
That porphyry whence grew the summer rose ;

For when spring comes, the dew with golden foot
Will touch the hidden leaf, the wrinkled root :

Then the grey dust that was the world's desire
Will sigh, ' Once I was wild and blind
In my desires as the snow. I loved where I list

And was violent like spring roots. . . . O might I feel
    again
The violence, the uproar of bursting buds, the wild-beast
    fire

Of spring in my veins — and know again the kiss
That holds all the spring redness and the rose that weeps
    in the blood —
O might I know but this ! '

Song

THE Queen Bee sighed, ' How heavy is my sweet gold,'
To the wind in the honey-hive.
And sighed the old King, ' The weight of my crown is
    cold —
And laden is life ! '
' How heavy,' sighed the gold heart of the day, ' is the
    heat ! '
Ah, not so laden sweet
As my heart with its infinite gold and its weight of love.

Girl and Butterfly

I, AN old man,
Bent like Ixion on my broken wheel the world,
Stare at the dust and scan
What has been made of it . . . and my companion

Shadow, born with a wolfish pelt —
Grey dress to wear against the invincible cold
Sits at my feet. . . . We scan the old
And young, we stare at the old woman
Who bears a stone in her breast
That will not let her rest
Because it once was a world in the grey dawn
When sap and blood were one.

We stare at the young girl chasing a yellow butterfly
On the summer roads that lead from Nothing to Nowhere.

What golden racers, young winds, have gone !   For the
        dust like a great wave
Breaks over them — the shade of mortality lying
On the golden hand (the calyx outshining all flowers) —
The hand that drew the chart of the undiscovered,
And the smile for which great golden heroes marched
        with the pride
And pomp of waves — and like the waves they died.
The words that drew from the shade
A planetary system :
                    These are gone —

And the Grey Man that waits on the Road from Nothing
        to Nowhere
Does not care how the breezes and butterflies move their
        four wings —
And now the old woman who once was a world and my
        earth,
Lies like time upon my heart, or a drift of the grey dust.

But the young girl chases the yellow butterfly
Happiness . . . what is the dust that lies on its wings ?
Is it from far away
From the distance that lies between lover and lover, their
    minds never meeting —
Like the bright continents ? — are Asia, Africa, and
    Cathay
But golden flowers that shine in the fields of summer —
As quickly dying ?

'Green Flows the River of Lethe—O'

GREEN flows the river of Lethe — O
Long Lethe river
Where the fire was in the veins — and grass is growing
Over the fever —
The green grass growing. . . .

I stood near the Cities of the Plains
And the young girls were chasing their hearts like the gay
    butterflies
Over the fields of summer —
O evanescent velvets fluttering your wings
Like winds and butterflies on the Road from Nothing to
    Nowhere !

But in the summer drought
I fled, for I was a Pillar of Fire, I was Destruction
Unquenched, incarnate and incarnadine.

I was Annihilation
Yet white as the Dead Sea, white as the Cities of the Plains.
For I listened to the noontide and my veins
That threatened thunder and the heart of roses.

I went the way I would —
But long is the terrible Street of the Blood
That had once seemed only part of the summer redness :
It stretches for ever, and there is no turning
But only fire, annihilation, burning.

I thought the way of the Blood would never tire
But now only the red clover
Lies over the breath of the lion and the mouth of the
    lover —

And green flows Lethe river — O
Long Lethe river
Over Gomorrah's city and the fire. . . .

28

O yet forgive

O YET forgive my heart in your long night !
I am too poor to be Death's self so I might lie
Upon your heart . . . for my mortality
Too sad and heavy is, would leave a stain
Upon young lips, young eyes. . . . You will not
    come again :
So the weight of Atlas' woe, changed to a stone,
And that stone is my heart, I laid above
Your eyes, till blind as love
You no more see the work of the old wise.

But you in your long night are not deceived :
And so, not heeding the world, you let it roll
Into the long abyss
And say, ' What is that sound ? I am alone. . . .
Is it my great sunrise ? '

A Mother to her Dead Child

THE winter, the animal sleep of the earth is over
And in the warmth of the affirming sun
All beings, beasts, men, planets, waters, move
Freed from the imprisoning frost, acclaim their love
That is the light of the sun.

                     So the first spring began
Within the heart before the Fall of Man.

The earth puts forth its sprays, the heart its warmth,
And your hands push back the dark that is your nurse,
Feel for my heart as in the days before your birth.
O Sun of my life, return to the waiting earth
Of your mother's breast, the heart, the empty arms.
Come soon, for the time is passing, and when I am old
The night of my body will be too thick and cold
For the sun of your growing heart.   Return from your
    new mother
The earth : she is too old for your little body,
Too old for the small tendernesses, the kissings
In the soft tendrils of your hair.   The earth is so old
She can only think of darkness and sleep, forgetting
That children are restless like the small spring shadows.
But the huge pangs of winter and the pain
Of the spring's birth, the endless centuries of rain
Will not lay bare your trusting smile, your tress,
Or lay your heart bare to my heart again
In your small earthly dress.
And when I wait for you upon the summer roads
They bear all things and men, business and pleasure,
    sorrow,
And lovers' meetings, mourning shades, the poor man's
    leisure,
And the foolish rose that cares not ever for the far to-
    morrow.
But the roads are too busy for the sound of your feet,
And the lost men, the rejected of life, who tend the wounds

That life has made as if they were a new sunrise, whose
    human speech is dying
From want, to the rusted voice of the tiger, turn not their
    heads lest I hear your child-voice crying
In that hoarse tiger-voice : ' I am hungry ! am cold ! '
Lest I see your smile upon lips that were made for the kiss
    that exists not,
The food that deserts them, — those lips never warm with
    love, but from the world's fever,
Whose smile is a gap into darkness, the breaking apart
Of the long-impending earthquake that waits in the heart.
That smile rends the soul with the sign of its destitution,
It drips from the last long pangs of the heart, self-devouring,
And tearing the seer.

                      Yet one will return to the lost men,
Whose heart is the Sun of Reason, dispelling the shadow
That was born with no eyes to shed tears, — bringing peace
    to the lust
And pruriency of the Ape, from the human heart's sublimity
And tenderness teaching the dust that it is holy,
And to those who are hungry, are naked and cold as the
    worm, who are bare as the spirit
In that last night when the rich and the poor are alone,
Bringing love like the daily bread, like the light at morning.
And knowing this, I would give you again, my day's darling,
My little child who preferred the bright apple to gold,
And who lies with the shining world on his innocent eyes,
Though night-long I feel your tears, bright as the rose
In its sorrowful leaves, on my lips, and feel your hands
Touching my cheek, and wondering ' Are those your tears ? '
O grief, that your heart should know the tears that seem
    empty years
And the worlds that are falling !

Holiday

O you, all life, and you, the primal Cause —
The Sun and Planets to the husbandman,
The kernel and the sap, the life-blood, flower
Of all that lives, the Power
That holds the Golden Rainers in the heaven,

The wasteful Gardener Who to grow one flower —
Your life, like a long-petalled Sun, has strewn the infinite
Meadow of space with calyxes that die
Like dew, has sown the seed of this hour that comes no
    more —
Growing in Time, too thin as an abstraction
Yet holding in the end our bones like winter.

Come, we will leave the grey life, the half light
Where we are like the blind, live but in Time
When Toil, the arithmetician, rules the beat
Of blood and heart.
              Beneath the flowering boughs of heaven
The country roads are made of thickest gold —
They stretch beyond the world, and light like snow
Falls where we go, the Intelligible Light
Turns all to gold, the apple, the dust, the unripe wheat-ear.
Young winds and people have winged feet like Mercury,
And distance is dead, the world ends in the heart.

On this great holiday
Dives and Lazarus are brothers again :
They seem of gold as they come up from the city
Casting aside the grave-clothes of their lives
Where the ragged dust is nobly born as the Sun.
Now Atlas lays aside his dying world,
The clerk, the papers in the dusty office ;
And lovers meet their bright Antipodes
To whom they are borne by the young siren seas
Of blood . . . he finds no more his dark night is her noon,

For they forget their minds' polarity,
The jarring atoms. . . . The least ore of gold
And quality of dust
Holds a vein of holiness . . . the laws that lie
In the irrefutable dust are Fate's decrees.
No more is Man
The noonday hope of the worm that is his brother —
He who begins with the shape of that eyeless one
Then changes to the world in the mother's side :
For the heart of Man is yet unwearied by Chaos,
And the hands grown thumbless from unuse, the work-
    less hands
Where the needs of famine have grown the claws of the
    lion
Bear now on their palms the wounds of the Crucified.

For now the unborn God in the human heart
Knows for a moment all sublimities. . . .
Old people at evening sitting in the doorways
See in a broken window of the slum
The Burning Bush reflected, and the crumb
For the starving bird is part of the broken Body
Of Christ Who forgives us — He with the bright Hair
— The Sun Whose Body was spilt on our fields to bring
    us harvest.

NOTES

GREEN SONG

Page 4, line 17

' " I wept for names, sounds, faiths, delights, and duties lost " :
taken from a poem on Cowley's wish to retire to the Plantations.'
—Dorothy Wordsworth, *Grasmere Journal*, May 8, 1802.

A YOUNG GIRL

Page 8, line 5

An adaptation from a line in Rilke's ' Venus '.

HARVEST

Page 10, lines 8, 9, and 10

' It is obvious that the heat contained in animals is not fire, neither
does it derive its origin from fire ' : Aristotle, quoted by William
Harvey (*The Works of William Harvey, M.D.*, translated from the
Latin by R. Willis, Sydenham Society, 1842).   Harvey continues :
' I maintain the same thing of the innate heat and the blood : I say
that they are not fire and neither do they derive their origin from fire.
They rather share the nature of some other, and that a more divine
body and substance.   They act by no faculty or property of the
elements . . . as, in producing an animal, it ' (the generative factor)
' surpasses the power of the elements — as it is a spirit, namely, and
the inherent nature of that spirit corresponds to the essence of the
stars, so is there a spirit, or certain force, inherent in the blood, acting
superiorly to the power of the elements.'

Page 10, lines 17 and 18

' The inferior world, according to Aristotle, is so continuous and
connected with the superior orbits, that all its motions and changes
appear to take their rise and to receive directions from thence. . . .
Inferior and corruptible things wait upon superior and incorruptible
things ; but all are subservient to the will of the supreme, omni-
potent, and eternal creator.'—*Ibid.*

Page 10, lines 28 and 29

' Best is water of all, and gold as a flaming sun in the night shineth
eminent.'—Pindar.

Page 11, lines 17 to 19

' He gives us men for an refreshment the bread of angels. . . .
On the breaking of the Bread Thou art not broken, nor art Thou

34

divided. Thou art eaten, but like the Burning Bush, Thou art not consumed.'—St. Thomas Aquinas, *Sermon of the Body of Our Lord.*

ONE DAY IN SPRING

Page 16, *line* 17

' And in the spring night they must sleep alone.'—An adaptation of a line by Sappho.

INVOCATION

Page 18, *lines* 26 to 29

' The blood, when present in the veins as part of a body, a generative part, too, and endowed with soul, being the soul's immediate instrument, and primary seat . . . the blood, seeming also to have a share of another divine body and being suffused with divine animal heat, suddenly acquires remarkable and most excellent powers, and is analogous to the essence of the stars. In so far as it is spirit, it is the hearth, the Vesta, the household divinity, the innate heat, the sun of the microcosm, the fire of Plato ; not because like common fire it lightens, burns and destroys, but because, by a vague and incessant motion it preserves, nourishes and aggrandizes itself. It further deserves the name of spirit, inasmuch as it is radical moisture, at once the ultimate and the proximate and the primary aliment.'—William Harvey, *op. cit.*

'LO, THIS IS SHE THAT WAS THE WORLD'S DESIRE'

Page 22, *line* 22

' Venus. . . .' I used the name merely as a symbol. This poem is not about a far-away myth. . . . It is equally, let us say, about the girl who once walked under the flowering trees in the garden next door, and who is now old and bent, waiting for death in a shuttered house. . . . It is about all beauty gone.

GIRL AND BUTTERFLY

Page 26, *line* 25

'. . . how Butterflies and breezes move their four wings. . . .' —Sir Thomas Browne, ' The Garden of Cyrus '.

HOLIDAY

Page 32, *line* 19

' God is Intelligible Light.'—St. Thomas Aquinas, *Summa Theologiae.*

35

Printed in Great Britain by R. & R. CLARK, LIMITED, *Edinburgh.*